NICKISMS

ALL YOU NEED TO KNOW ABOUT MANAGING AN ENTRPRENEURIAL BUSINESS

Nick Stanfield

NICKISMS:
ALL YOU NEED TO KNOW ABOUT MANAGING AN ENTREPRENEURIAL BUSINESS

© 1996 Nick Stanfield

Published by Adriel Publishing

www.adrielpublishing.com

SECOND EDITION

Printed in the U.S.A.

ISBN: 978-1-892324-49-8

NICKISMS:

ALL YOU NEED TO KNOW ABOUT MANAGING AN ENTREPRENEURIAL BUSINESS

A Collection of Nickisms that can form the core foundation for successfully managing your own entrepreneurial operation.

Nick Stanfield

ACKNOWLEDGEMENTS

I am personally grateful for the many people in my life, family, friends and business associates, who have made my life better, richer and stronger for having been there.

A special thanks to Pat Kilpatrick

INTRODUCTION TO NICKISMS

Nickisms are mostly anecdotal "words to live by" that I have collected over the years. Some are perceived to be original, others I have picked up from friends. Where I can give credit, I always do, even if it is only where I first saw or heard the "ism".

Some of my acquaintances suggest my upbringing in rural North Carolina lay the groundwork of my "ism" as only a colloquialism of a "red neck". It could be, but I'll let you be the judge of that.

As a student and analyst, first of large corporations and later the entrepreneurial enterprise of managers and management technique, I have come to realize that there are many roads to success. Many noted business scholars have written about management philosophy, or the fad of the moment that is: the ultimate in how to run a successful company. I personally believe that each individual has to develop his or her own management philosophy and guidelines that work for the individual. Just as there is no right way to hit a baseball – do what is comfortabe with your management style.

The Nickisms presented herein are given as "business truths" which will allow you to develop the core foundation for the successful management of your business.

I hope you find a grain or two of truth, humor, and assistance in this book. Remember, no architect ever attempts to design a building without developing a detailed blueprint, no contractor tries to build a building without that blueprint, no banker ever makes a loan on the building without a review and analysis of that blueprint, and no investor ever buys the building without having seen those blueprints.

Does it not stand to reason that if you are going to build a successful and viable business you are going to be required to develop your blueprint (i.e., a formal business plan) and execute that plan with your own management philosophy.

I hope my Nickisms help.

TABLE OF CONTENTS

NICKISM 1

"My fear is not of trying and failing but rather of not trying and being less than I might have been."

NICKISM 1

This is my favorite "ism". However, I have seen the point made in other statements.

I have been the founder or co-founder of seven start-up companies. Three died and went to heaven and four grew up to be bigger than a bread box. I think all true entrepreneurs are driven by some internal force to reach a little higher on the economic ladder.

I doubt any think of failing as they start out to create a new company, and often it may be the loss of other employment that pushes an entrepreneur to take that first step. But, my bet is the internal drive is there and the thought of only being someone else's "shoe clerk" and being less of an individual success than possible is there for most entrepreneurs.

NICKISM 2

"Life is about: High moral values, honesty, integrity and ethics."

"There is no right way to do a wrong thing."

(In the office of Ned Boshell,
President of Columbia General Corporation)

NICKISM 2

These two "isms" are about people, you and me, if you will. Are we good decent human beings or are we something less. Money is not good or bad per se, only in how it is used. If in our drive for success, we cut corners, step on the scales, speak with a forked tongue, or down right cheat someone, then we have failed in life even if we have economic success.

NICKISM 3

*"There are three kinds of discipline:
spiritual, physical and mental."*

NICKISM 3

For the religious person, he or she must consistently practice spiritual correctness to be accepted into the Kingdom of God.

For the athlete to win the marathon, he or she must consistently train to stay in shape to run a good race.

The mental muscle must be consistently exercised and trained if we expect to respond to the challenges of profitably managing a business in today's environment.

The point is to suggest that we all would be better people and managers if we worked harder at staying in shape in all three areas.

NICKISM 4

"Anyone can start a business — only a few can build a business."

"The common thread of all successful people: They are doers."

NICKISM 4

In Texas alone, there are thousands of corporations chartered each year, and many do not make it. Probably most get no further than the first $1,000 required to incorporate. Starting the business is the easy part, building the business is something else. In Dallas, we have corporations such as: EDS (Ross Perot), Home Interiors and Gifts (Mary Carter-Crowley), Mary Kay Cosmetics (Mary Kay Ash), Sedco, Inc. (Bill Clements), Texas Instruments (Erik Jonsson) and many others. These companies were started from scratch by individuals with the drive to succeed.

The common thread of these and other very successful people is that they are doers. They didn't just talk about starting a business, they built one! With success, they were able to hire many employees, pay lots of taxes, be good corporate citizens, and create wealth for their shareholders.

NICKISM 5

"The correct corporate structure is the one which gives the company the optimum chance for success."

NICKISM 5

The correct corporate structure is normally given little analysis prior to starting a business. The first shoe is can I make enough to pay my economic needs (i.e., replace the salary I was making at my big company), the second shoe is I don't want to pay any taxes, and finally I am too busy to think about anything else.

Now let's take a look at the full "ism." The correct corporate structure is the one which gives the company the optimum chance for success. That is, take care of the company first and you can ultimately take care of the stockholders and management. My point is that too often an entrepreneur doesn't focus on the big picture until late in the game, often too late. The big picture should always be — how do I create the maximum market value in my business. Sometimes, you may have to reduce your salary by one dollar or pay one dollar in taxes to drive the market value up by one hundred dollars.

NICKISM 6

"Stockholder's equity is to the balance sheet as the foundation is to a building."

NICKISM 6

Everyone understands that the four inch slab that my house sits on will not support a ten story building. And yet, time and time again, entrepreneurs think they can build and operate a business with ten million dollars in annual revenue with a few thousand dollars in equity.

A company with too little equity will fail ninety-nine times out of one hundred. Why? Because without the adequate equity, the business will go under with the slightest hiccup. Now, I am not saying you have to have a million dollars in equity to start a business. What I am saying is you have to understand how much equity is required to support a certain level of annual revenue. The old axiom of *"you can go broke with too much business just as easy as with too little business"* is the principle of this "ism."

An entrpreneur thinks all he or she has to do is make the sale. They tend to overlook little things like dollars tied up in monthly overhead, inventory, and accounts receivable. Each entrepreneur should spend a lot of time studying and understanding his or her cash flow projections for the maximum and minimum level of revenue. It may surprise you as to what you find.

NICKISM 7

"The only things certain in life are: death, taxes and accelerated change."

NICKISM 7

Many years ago, the saying was "death and taxes." Then in the 1960's, we began to realize that "change" in our lives was beginning to take on a certain reality (i.e., the good old days would never be revisited). I am sure the progress in technology is the driving force in our lives of "accelerated change." The faster the computer chip processes data, the faster our lives change for bad or good.

In 1964, I was a young banker with First National Bank in Dallas (six or so changes later, we have Bank of America) attending a Texas Municipal Advisory Council seminar on the campus of Sam Houston State College. The main speaker at our closing dinner gave a very interesting, funny, and thought-provoking presentation on change since the beginning of time. His main theme was that since the beginning of modern man (i.e., 2000 B.C.) until about 1900 our technology had made very little progress. From 1900 until 1940, the curve of his chart began to show a steady rise. From 1940 until the present (i.e., 1964), the graph was a true spike upward. I have often wondered if the man is still giving his same speech, and if he is, what does his chart look like today. As sure as I am writing this book, the change in our world will continue to accelerate and how we deal with it in our personal lives, as well as our businesses will separate the winner from the "also rans." Don't fight "accelerated change" because it is just as inevitable as "death and taxes."

NICKISM 8

"Management is like a three legged milk stool: to have a successful business you must sell it, make it (or have it made) and manage it."

NICKISM 8

The essence of building a business is about managing efficiently. The normal physiological profile of an entrepreneur is salesman: first, second and last. As I tell many of our clients, if it takes you twenty-four hours a day making it and selling it, you had better invent another twelve hours for managing it.

Too often, the entrepreneur starts a business and can be successful as long as that company only has annual revenue of one million dollars. Why? Because the owner/manager can run it out of his hip pocket. Only when sales start to have significant growth does the operation get out of control. Why? Because the entrepreneur resists building a management team, assigning and delegrating responsibilities, having formal policies and procedures, and in short — bulding a company.

NICKISM 9

"Recognition and flexibility are
the keys to successful management."

NICKISM 9

Recognition and flexibility are the primary keys to successful management of almost everything. From investment management to business management, you have to be able to recognize change when it begins to occur and then to be flexible in your own thinking to adapt to that change. For some time, the debate over the world economy versus the local economy has raged. Let me set the record straight. If you think your business is only governed by local economics, you are doomed to fail.

Several years ago, the mushroom farmers in Western Pennsylvania thought their geographic location protected them from any domestic competition. Then, Pepsi Cola announced a deal with the government of China, Pepsi syrup for mushrooms (PepsiCo's Pizza Hut uses a lot of mushrooms).

Always be on your intellectual toes looking for change and be ready to adapt.

NICKISM 10

"Always manage with the maximum elasticity of overhead."

NICKISM 10

Maximum Elasticity of Overhead ("MEO") – is it an adverb, an adjective or a management philosophy?

First, let's look at the individual words. Maximum is defined as the greatest amount possible. Elasticity is defined as the ability to change in direct response to a force. Overhead is defined as the general cost of running a business. The dictionary might then define "Maximum Elasticity of Overhead" as a metaphor if not an oxymoron.

I will use maximum elasticity of overhead as a management philosophy and a vital element in the entrepreneur's survival kit. Overhead is most often referred to as "fixed overhead" which by definition and history are our operating costs which repeat themselves every month without fail and without any regard to that particular month's revenues. Why most of us were taught this concept is beyond me. Look at history and ask the question, "Why don't empires survive, why don't professional sports teams repeat as champions, and why don't successful businesses endure? My answer is they get fat. Fat of mind, spirit and body. The sucessful business of yesterday lets too many costs slip from variable expenses to fixed expenses.

I attended a lunch once where the speaker, a psychologist, discussed the organizational life cycle. His message was that being an adult was great, the best time of all, we only needed programs to keep fit. I suggest and recommend that if you commit to the management philosophy of "Maximum Elasticity of Overhead," you will stay fit, survive and prosper.

NICKISM 11

"There are three equal ingredients to each sale: you must make the sale, deliver the product or service and get the money in the bank."

NICKISM 11

The salesman in us often thinks: getting the order is the end of the game. Not true! The product or service must be made and delivered on time and on budget. Finally, the invoice must be paid with good funds and deposited in the bank.

How many of us have had an "ace salesman" say, big company has been around for one hundred years so they must be a good credit risk.

How many times has the "ace salesman" made a sale and changed the product just enough to drive the cost of production through the roof.

Policies that freeze manufacturing design and make credit a selling tool normally allow a good sale to occur.

NICKISM 12

"Always be hungry — always
run scared."

NICKISM 12

I was given this advice by a USAF Tech Sergeant as a very young airman back in 1957 while stationed at Carswell Air Force Base in Fort Worth, Texas. It was good advice then; it's even better advice now.

"Always be hungery" tells me I should never be satisfied with my performance or production if I know I can improve myself. Just because I closed a transaction today doesn't mean there is not another transaction for me to work on tomorrow.

"Always run scared" because someone may be gaining on you. No matter how good you are, if you slow down just a bit or lose just a bit of your sharp edge, someone will take away your trophy.

NICKISM 13

"Rewards are for results not effort."

(Plaque in the office of John L. Austin,
Vice President–Equipment and Maintenance,
FFE Transportation Services, Inc.)

NICKISM 13

This "ism" answers one of my favorite rhetorical questions. If you push on the wall all day and the wall does not move, have you done any work? The answer is a simple "no": the wall did not move, and while you may have expended energy you did not do anything.

So as not to get on my political soapbox, I'll confine any comparisons to professional athletes. I pass my time on Sundays watching pro football and have observed how much the pro athlete congratulates himself just for showing up. I read about a young man who was about to enter the NBA and thought his services were worth $100 million before he ever produced one basket, much less one NBA championship. The 1994 baseball strike was truly amazing in that ballplayers wanted to negotiate individual contracts for millions but then strike as a team over other matters.

NICKISM 14

"The acceptable standard of performance should be how well we did against how well we should have done."

NICKISM 14

How many of us lower our standard when we say, and accept, the industry norm is "X." Yes, we should study and analyze industry ratios to know what our competition is. However, if I make one million dollars and I could have, and should have, made two million dollars for that year or transaction, did I do a good job? I think not.

Doing a good job and measuring that performance should always be: how well I did against how well I should have done.

NICKISM 15

*"Never do business with a man or
woman who will lie to you.
Because, sooner or later, he or she
will lie to himself or herself
and he or she will truly become lost."*

NICKISM 15

How often do we hear that "little white lie" from our sales department that the "big" order is about to come in. That "big" order seldom is real, and too many companies get in trouble building a business deal on blue sky.

Find a few good men and women who are always open and honest with each other, and I will show you the making of a strong management team which can build a company to great heights.

NICKISM 16

"The best of pets and friends will ultimately bite the hand that feeds them: solution always wear a steel glove."

NICKISM 16

This "ism" is a bit of a downer. However, it is important to remember that, in management, you normally cannot be an employee's best friend.

In the military, they have a non-fraternizaton policy between officers and enlisted men. Is this a good policy in business? I'll leave that up to you. But remember, never let personal feelings interfere with a good business decision.

NICKISM 17

"We are all on commission no matter the title of our compensation."

NICKISM 17

How interesting it is to hear people justify why they are worth $X. I need $X because I have five kids or I have a big house payment. I don't care! Tell me how much you will produce for my company, and I'll tell you how much I'll pay you. It is truly refreshing to interview an individual and he or she understands that the only basis for his or her compensation package is how much they produce (i.e., they are on commission).

Now, I am the first to admit it is easier to write a commission formula for the sales department than the rest of the staff. I have been looking for that secret formula for thirty years. However, I am committed to developing plans, and evaluating performance of said plans, that pay everyone for their performance. In my opinion, the optimum pay/incentive plan is to get all employees to commit to the game plan by: (1) putting everyone on the same page; (2) everyone thinking like owners; and (3) everyone being rewarded for the same results.

NICKISM 18

"Business is about making a profit."

"Gentlemen, let me remind you we are in the busines of making money; we incidentally sell steel."

(John Mahar, President of Metal Services, Inc.)

"The only way to be secure is to make money and generate cash. Everythng else is a means to that end."

(Jack Stack, President of Springfield Remanufacturing Corporation.)

NICKISM 18

Business is about making a profit. This is the last "ism" and the most important. Early in this little book, we talked about what life is about so everyone reading this message would know how high I place moral values, honest, integrity and ethics.

But, I want to leave you with how strongly I feel about making a profit. For without profits, nothing else happens. As Jack Stack, President of Springfield Remanufacturing Corporation says in his book: *The Great Game of Business*, the only way to be secure is to make money.

Let's examine what being secure means. First, if a company is profitable, its employees are secure that they will continue to have employment and will be able to provide for their families.

Second, with profits, a company can continue to grow by adding an additional plant and equipment. It is true if you are not growing, you are dying.

Third, only a profitable company can be a good corporate citizen. If your company is not profitable, how do you give back to your community.

Fourth, if a company is profitable, it will pay taxes. This is not necessarily a bad thing. No matter how bad our politicians are, our government is still the best there is and deserves our support. And, don't forget, for every 34 cents in taxes, a company gets to keep 66 cents in retained earnings. Retained earnings are the foundation of a company. The foundation, just like a building, allows you to build a bigger company because your foundation grows stronger with each dollar of retained earnings.

Fifth, and finally, a profitable company can reward its shareholders with a more valuable investment. The only reason for an investor to put money in your company is the expectation that the value of each share will improve over time. Even if you are the only shareholder, you should have that same expectation. The current buzz phrase "creating shareholder value" does not only apply to the Fortune 500 companies.

Profits are not a dirty word, and each and every entrepreneur should stand and defend profits as the cornerstone of the American free enterprise system. I will debate anyone — anywhere — that without profits my company — your company — all companies will wither and die and so will the USA.

EIGHT KEYS TO SUCCESSFUL MANAGEMENT

1. Manage the business with and against an operating business plan. Cash flow and capital requirements analysis are critical.

2. Manage the business with maximum elasticity of overhead and plan with zero based budgeting.

3. Use monthly variance reports to monitor performance.

4. Have all employees on some form of incentive plan.

5. Work hard at developing banking relationships.

6. Work hard at developing vendor relationships.

7. Remember that the customer is not always right ... but, he or she is always the customer.

8. The only reason to be in business is to make money, you incidentally sell X.

ABOUT THE AUTHOR

Nick Stanfield is the Founder, President and CEO of MSI Capital Corporation, a Dallas-based investment banking firm specializing in financial management, corporate finance and investment banking services to private entre-preneurial companies. MSI Capital was organized in 1976 and operated until 2016.

Stanfield has been the founder or co-founder of seven operating companies and has invested in another nineteen private companies. MSI Capital has assisted clients secure outside funding of over $100 million since 1976.

MSI Capital has provided financial management services to clients ranging in size from start-up to $50 million in annual revenues.

Stanfield is a graduate of the University of North Texas (BBA-1963), Denton, Texas. He served in banking for six years as an Investment and Trust Officer and with regional investment banking firms as a Vice President for seven years before founding MSI Capital Corporation.

Stanfield is available to speak on this or other entreprenuerial and financial subjects. He can be reached via email at: nicks6668@gmail.com or by phone at: 214-415-9223.

Note: If you or your organization would like quantity discounts of the download (pdf) or the paperback version of this book, please contact me at the email or phone number above.

NOTES

NOTES

NOTES

NOTES

www.ingramcontent.com/pod-product-compliance
Lightning Source LLC
Chambersburg PA
CBHW060054050426
42448CB00011B/2446